Teach Yourself
Torchon Lace

EUNICE ARNOLD

Teach Yourself Torchon Lace

6 basic lessons in bobbin lace with workcards

RUTH BEAN
Carlton Bedford

Published by Ruth Bean, Victoria Farmhouse, Carlton, Bedford
MK43 7LP, England.

Cover design, James Butler, linocut by Sylvia Worthington.

Printed in Great Britain at the
University Press, Cambridge, England.

FOREWORD

Eunice Arnold's lace making method has been well tried on many pupils including me. Some nine years ago, when I was responsible for researching and producing new editions of several lace classics — Maidment, Mincoff & Marriage, etc., which were then out of print, I asked her to teach me. My self-satisfaction at quickly picking up the technique was somewhat damped by Mrs Arnold who said "Don't let it go to your head, me duck: I teach children and they make lace like this too!"

Since then I have observed with pleasure the growing interest in lace making and other crafts, but have always felt there was room for an original book designed for convenient and effective use by the beginner taking up lace without ready access to a teacher. The book has been produced with this in mind. The method has been carefully revised and supplemented by special working cards and the text read critically by others.

I would like to thank particularly Mrs Arnold for her enthusiasm and patience and Mrs Kathy Jones of Emberton, Bucks, for her helpful comments.

Ruth Bean

To the memory of Dad, John Lemuel Arnold, 1890 to 1968, who said it couldn't be done

CONTENTS

INTRODUCTION

My Great Aunt Liz was a lacemaker, but she died before I was old enough to learn. Granny Arnold was a lacemaker, but she died before I was old enough even to think of joining her family. But lace was in the blood on both sides of the family and I was determined to learn. I had my equipment ready and there were still two months before the evening classes started. I got all the books I could from the library and decided to make a start. That was when Dad made his famous statement: "It can't be done. No one has ever learned to make lace from a book. You have to be shown." That did it! I worked for hours. The result was very poor and was eventually thrown away.

Mrs Benson, my first lace teacher, soon had me hard at work on a wide variety of patterns. I contracted the 'Lace Disease' and rapidly became an incurable addict. But as time went on, I began to realise that the technique did not come as easily to some people as it did to others, so I began to work out a series of patterns that would solve this problem. Family, friends and children at school were subjected to concentrated doses of various patterns and their reactions observed. Eventually I settled for the six patterns I have used in this book. They have served me well and many of my former pupils have used them successfully in classes they have run.

Over the years I have found, whether my pupil has been five or seventy five, that the reaction has been the same: the first piece of lace has been most important. This is why I dispense with the 'practice strips' and start everyone on a piece of Ground work, which can be used as a simple decoration.

Many people will say that Torchon lace should not be encouraged and that using it for beginners will put them off learning the more intricate and delicate forms of lace. As a child, my very first piece of knitting was a dish cloth (torchon in French) done in garter stitch. Mother used it for months and I was very proud of it. If I hadn't knitted my first dish cloth, my husband would not now be wearing Aran sweaters. Many people I know and have taught get great pleasure from making Torchon lace, some because they can't see well enough to make the finer laces and others because they haven't the time to sit and apply the concentration demanded by more intricate patterns.

Only one stitch is used in this book, Full stitch. I have found that the introduction of Half stitch too soon causes great confusion. There are other things I have missed out too, like the extra pair to make a footside, because they have caused trouble to people working alone. Lacemakers will be quick to point out these matters, but I have not written this book for the lacemaker, I have written out these lessons for people who want to learn to make lace but don't know another lacemaker and can't reach a class. I have made the instructions as full as possible so that, if needs be, father can read them out while mother makes the lace!

To my children in class I say "There is no such thing as can't. Try and you will find you can." To those of you who are going to try, I wish good luck.

I wish to thank all members of my family who have suffered as guinea pigs in my various schemes, but especially Aunt Hamish, my first pupil, and my nieces Tilda, Karen and Sarah, who have worked principally from my written instructions. My thanks also go to the many people I have taught over the years; they have played their part in adding to my experience, and some are even now using my basic instruction for their own pupils.

Finally I must thank Ruth Bean, for her unswerving faith in me, and the many hours she has spent checking every word in the book, making sure that she could see clearly how the lace is to be made.

Eunice Arnold, September 1979

MATERIALS NEEDED

You need: a pillow, bobbins, thread, pins, a pattern, some card, a pricker, a pin cushion, and two cover cloths.

Cover cloths need to be made from material which is easy to look at: blue or green are the best colours, and cotton or linen the best material. If you make them specially, they need to be approximately 18 inches (46 cm) square. I use my fancy souvenir tea towels, as the long end can be pulled up over the bobbins and lace at packing up time.

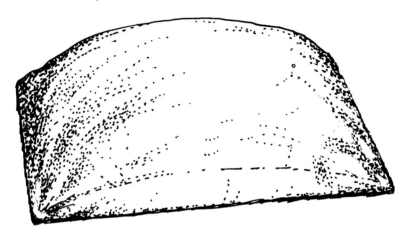

lace pillow

MAKING A LACE PILLOW

First of all find a piece of board about 16 inches (40 cm) square (but that piece in the shed is just what you want so long as it is not less than 12 inches (30 cm) square).

Next find a piece of strong material, any sort so long as it is tough: calico, twill, canvas, sacking, linen union, ticking; plain or patterned makes no difference. Make the material into a bag so that the board will just slide into it, and leave about six inches spare at the open end, for sewing up. If I had a board 16 inches square, I would make my bag the size of a pillowcase.

The next job is to get some straw. If you have never made a pillow before, decide how much straw you think you will need to fill the pillow, and then go out and get three times that amount! The straw seems to melt when you start the job of stuffing the pillow.

Shops and warehouses dealing with glass usually have some straw, if there is no farm near you. Wood wool can also be used. Sawdust will make a very heavy pillow, and will cause trouble for anyone who suffers from hay fever and such like complaints. Stuffing used for household pillows and cushions will not pack tightly enough to hold the pins. A block of polystyrene packing, or several ceiling tiles stuck together, will make a temporary pillow.

Stuffing a straw pillow needs strong arms. Enlist help if you can. First of all, dampen the straw slightly, as this helps you pack it more tightly. Put the board in its bag, then take a handful of straw and ram it hard into the corners of the bag, on one side of the board only. Use a rolling pin, mallet or hammer handle to ram the straw down hard. Hold the ends of the bag tightly, and bang hard on top of the pillow to pack the straw down. Put in more straw, ram it down, and then bang it hard on top. Continue in this way, until the bag is stretched really tight, and the straw is packed into a hard domed shape.

Now sew up the middle of the opening, pulling the ends of the bag over tightly. When this is done, poke more straw into the two corners with the handle of your hammer. When you are quite sure you cannot get another wisp of straw in, sew up the corners tightly. Leave the pillow a day or two for the straw to dry out. Remember: the harder your pillow, the easier it is to work, and the better the lace at the finish, because the pins will not move. If your finger is painfully sore after you have made a few inches of lace, you will know that you have made your pillow well.

BOBBINS

The traditional bobbin is made from wood or bone. It is approximately four inches (10 cm) long, and about as thick as a pencil. The short neck or head is for holding the loop, which prevents the thread which is wound round the long neck from unwinding. The spangle is made up of seven beads, preferably glass, to weight the bobbins and help keep the thread taut. The beads are threaded on to brass wire and attached to the bobbin through the hole in the shank. A handyman with a lathe can easily turn bobbins from quarter inch (6mm) dowelling, but make sure the neck and head are very smooth, so that the thread does not catch. Enterprising youngsters can whittle bobbins from small pieces of wood or sticks. If all else fails, old toothbrushes can be converted into makeshift bobbins by pulling out the bristles and winding the thread on the 'neck' below the 'head'. The loop to hold the thread will have to go on to this neck as well.

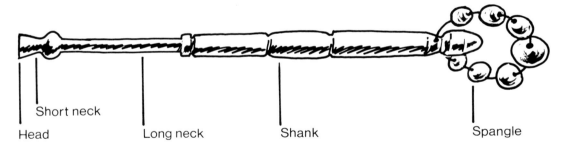

Short neck

Head   Long neck   Shank   Spangle

Winding the bobbin

The bobbins are wound in pairs when beginning a new pattern. This saves having a double quantity of ends to sew in when the lace is finished. Take a piece of thread about two or three yards long. The amount of thread you wind on to a bobbin will depend on the thickness of the thread and the size of the piece to be worked. If possible, it is better not to have to join in new threads while working the lace. Hold the bobbin in your left hand with the head pointing towards you. Wind the thread clockwise round the long neck of the bobbin. After making two or three turns of thread round the long neck,

7

continue winding by twisting the bobbin between your fingers. This prevents the thread twisting and knotting. When half the thread is on the bobbin, put a loop on the short neck to hold the thread (see below). Start at *the other end of the thread* and wind another bobbin in the same way. When there is about six inches of thread between the two bobbins, put a loop on the second bobbin. Wind enough pairs of bobbins in this way to start the pattern.

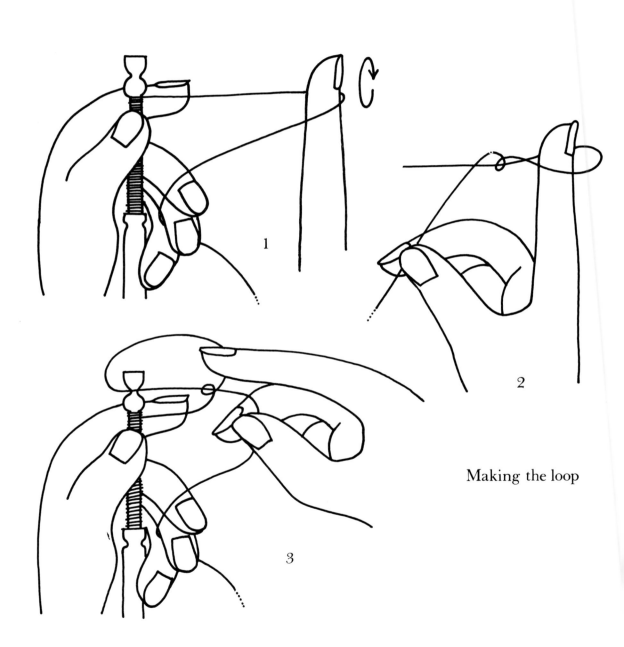

Making the loop

Making the loop

This loop is really a half hitch, for those of you who have been Guides or Scouts. For those of you who knit it is one stitch cast on thumb-method. If you do not know how to do either of these, make a long loose loop using about six inches (15 cm) of thread from the bobbin. Hold the bobbin and the thread in the same hand. Put the index finger of the other hand through the loop, twist the finger right round so that a small loop is made round the finger and then slip this loop on to the short neck of the bobbin. The loop will hold the thread in place while you are working. When you need more thread, hold the bobbin sideways, head to the left, and gently turn against the pull of the loop to unwind a little more thread. Do not have more than three inches (7 cm) of thread between the bobbin and the pins.

THREAD AND PINS

Lace was originally made from fine linen thread. Cotton threads were used later to compete with the price of machine made lace. Today there are many kinds of thread available but the linen thread, which still makes the best lace, is not very easy to obtain. Specially made brass pins which do not rust, are available from suppliers of lace equipment.

A thread the thickness of a 40 crochet cotton needs coarse pins. This will make a heavy type of lace suitable for table mats, tray cloths etc.

A thread the thickness of 80 to 100 crochet cotton needs medium pins. This will make a lace suitable for handkerchief edgings and trimmings for garments.

A thread finer than 100 needs fine pins.

All the patterns in this book have been made for thread the thickness of 40 crochet cotton.

MAKING THE PATTERN

The pattern must be pricked out on to a piece of card. Specially made card can be used many times, but a thin piece of cardboard will do, although this will soon wear out.

Trace the pattern from the pricking on the working card. Stick the traced pattern on to the card with a piece of sellotape, and then with a No. 8 sewing needle, stuck eye first into a cork, or a pin vice, prick through the pattern on to the card. It is a good idea to put a piece of polystyrene or cork tile under the card when pricking the pattern. Check carefully that you have not missed a hole by holding the card up to the light. If you wish, you can cut the pricking diagram off the working card and use that.

Remove the pattern and ink the markings for the pattern on to the card.

FIRST PATTERN

Prick the first pattern on to a piece of card. Ink in the pattern by joining the holes together diagonally. When you work the pattern, these lines will be covered by threads — if not, then you will know something is wrong.

The pattern is worked in Full Stitch and is known as Torchon Ground, because it is the background stitch used in most Torchon patterns. It is worked in diagonal rows from right to left.

The row marked with the arrows is the last row worked before turning the corner.

To prepare

Make your pattern.

Cover the pillow with one of the cloths and pin it down.

Pin the pattern firmly on to the pillow with the corner as near to the centre of the pillow as possible. This will help to give the maximum space when turning the corner.

Pin the second cloth tightly across the pillow, about half way down the pattern. This will be moved down as the work progresses, and will prevent the threads catching on the pattern.

Wind six pairs of bobbins in thread about as thick as 40 crochet cotton. You will need approximately 60 coarse pins.

Starting the pattern (setting in)

Stick a pin into each of the holes on the first diagonal row (Nos. 1—5). Make them lean slightly backwards and the first and last slightly outwards as well. This helps to keep the shape of the lace, gives something firm to pull against and prevents the work moving up the pins away from the pillow.

Hang one pair of bobbins on each of the first four pins from the right, and two pairs on the last pin. Label your bobbins from right to left as follows: AB on pin 1 / CD on pin 2 / EF on pin 3 / GH on pin 4 / LJ and KL on pin 5.

Remember that we are going to work from right to left in diagonal rows. Use the pair AB on first pin and the pair CD on second pin to make the first stitch as follows:

   Pick up C in your left hand and put it over B.
   Pick up B in your left hand and A in your right hand.
   Put B over D and A over C (In one movement).
   Pick up D in your left hand and put it over A.

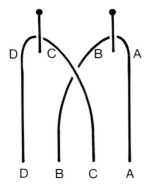

When you make this stitch without the labels you will see that what you really do is:

Cross the middle two threads once - left over right

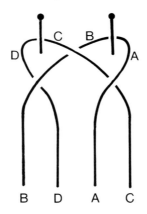

Twist the two side pairs of threads once - right over left

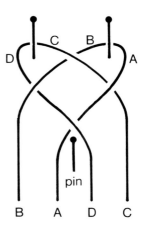

Cross the middle two threads once - left over right

This completes the stitch. It is called **Full Stitch** and is the basis of all lace making stitches. Every one of the pins used in this pattern is 'covered' by two of these stitches. Each large dot in the instructions below marks the beginning of the working of a new pinhole. If you look at the threads carefully you will see they have woven across each other as in a piece of material. Always watch the threads when working, and not the bobbins. The labels on the bobbins for this pattern are to help make things easier for the beginner, but watch the threads move and do away with the labels as soon as possible.

To continue

Separate the two pairs of bobbins (AB and CD) and put a pin in the first hole of the next row (No. 6) remembering to lean it slightly backwards. The stitch you have made is behind the pin with bobbins CD on the right and AB on the left; reading from right to left CDAB. Now cover the pin with the second stitch as follows:

Pick up A in your left hand and put it over D.

Pick up D in your left hand and C in the right hand.

Put D over B and C over A.

Pick up B in the left hand and put it over C.

The bobbins are now back in their original position. Pull up tightly to the pin. Twist both pairs twice to the left. That is:

A over B / B over A / C over D / D over C.

- Put the pair AB out of the way on the right of the pillow and move over the next pair EF to work the second hole with the pair CD.

E over D / D over F and C over E / F over C.

Lean a pin backwards in the second hole (No. 7).

C over F / F over D and E over C / D over E.

Twist both pairs twice:

C over D / D over C / E over F / F over E.

- Leave CD on the right side and bring in GH to work with EF.

G over F / F over H and E over G / H over E.

Lean a pin backwards in the third hole (No. 8).

E over H / H over F and G over E / F over G.

Twist both pairs twice:

E over F / F over E / G over H/ H over G.

- Leave EF on the right side and bring in IJ to work with GH.

I over H / H over J and G over I / J over G.

Lean a pin backwards in the fourth hole (No. 9).

G over J / J over H and I over G / H over I.

Twist both pairs twice:

G over H / H over G / I over J / J over I.

- Leave G H on the right side and bring in KL to work with IJ.

K over J / J over L and I over K / L over I.

Lean a pin backwards into the last hole (No. 10).

I over L / L over J and K over I / J over K.

Twist both pairs twice:

I over J / J over I / K over L / L over K.

This completes one row of ground. To get rid of the loops at the start of the lace take out pins 1 to 5, one at a time, and gently pull the pairs of bobbins in turn, until the loop is pulled down to the pins 6 to 10.

Move the bobbins carefully back to the left of the pillow and follow the same instructions for the next row, using holes 11 to 15. Continue in this way until you have completed the row marked with the arrows. Remember to pull all stitches up tightly to the pins, to make the lace firm.

When you have worked about three inches of this pattern begin to take out the pins from the back of the work, one at a time, to re-use them in the present working area.

The corner

When you have finished the row marked with the arrows turn the pillow round. Remembering that we work from right to left, looking at the lace from this side there appear to be five unfinished rows. Turning the corner means finishing these rows, as follows:

Work IJ and KL again (this will cover the single hole not used, No. 1).

Work GH and IJ then IJ and KL again to finish the next row (2 holes to cover: Nos 2, 3).

Work EF and GH / GH and IJ / IJ and KL again to finish the next row (3 holes to cover: Nos 4, 5, 6).

Work CD and EF / EF and GH / GH and IJ / IJ and KL to finish the next row (4 holes to cover: Nos 7, 8, 9, 10).

The next row is a complete row. Continue the pattern to the end of the pricking.

To set up (to move the work up the pattern to continue the lace)

Great care has to be taken at this stage to make sure that the weight of the bobbins does not fall on the lace and in consequence, draw it up.

Wrap all the bobbins up tightly in a cloth and pin the bundle so that the bobbins cannot move. Especially prevent them moving downwards.

Push the bundle up towards the lace so the thread between the bobbins and the end of the lace is slack. Pin the bundle very securely to the pillow. You will find hat pins very useful for this. When you are quite sure that neither the bobbins nor the bundle can move, then take out all the pins from the lace. Hold the bundle of bobbins in one hand and take out the pins holding it. Lift the bundle NOT THE LACE and move the work round to the beginning of the pattern. Pin the bundle of bobbins back on the pillow so that the first complete row of lace after the corner fits over the first row of holes at the beginning of the pattern. When the bundle is secure put the pins back into the lace, fitting it carefully back onto the pattern. When all the pins are firmly in place undo the bundle and continue working.

When four corners have been turned, work sufficient rows to give an overlap row for joining.

To join

Unwind 6 to 8 inches (15 to 20 cm) of thread from the bobbins and then cut the bobbins off. Using either a fine crochet hook or sewing needle, pull one thread from each pair hanging on the last row of stitches through the corresponding stitch on the first row. Tie the ends to hold them. Take out the pins. Undo the knots (no knots allowed in lace!) and use the ends of the threads to make a firm neat join, darning them in.

Alternatively, take the lace off the pillow and using a finer thread of the same type, stitch the first and last rows together. Darn in the ends of the lace, to make a firm join.

Mount the lace on the edge of a piece of cloth, or use it as a centre piece on a larger coloured cloth, so the colour of the cloth shows through the lace.

JOINING IN A NEW THREAD

Keep a watch for bobbins that are running out of thread, and save yourself a lot of darning in at the end. Wind another bobbin and hang it on a spare pin stuck in at the side of the pillow. When the old bobbin has just enough thread left on it to work with (about 6 to 7 inches) bring the new thread across to join it at a point where the old thread is at a pin. The pin will help to hold the new thread in place. Twist the new and the old threads together very tightly, then work on, using the two bobbins as though they were one, until this double thread has been round three pins. Untwist the threads and throw the old one back across the pillow. The bobbin will keep it out of the way, but cut the bobbin off before the pins are taken out at the join, or the weight of the bobbin will draw up the lace. The ends of both threads can be cut off close when the lace is finished.

If you break a thread close to the work, hang a new thread on a pin, lay it in place and continue working, but remember you must darn in the end of the new thread so that it holds the broken end in place. Do this before you mount your lace.

SECOND PATTERN

Prepare the pattern as before, by pricking it on to card and inking it in.
This pattern consists of a simple Fan worked in Full stitch with a twist, and four rows of Torchon Ground: the first row has 5 pin-holes to work (except when setting in and the first Ground after the corner, where there are only four as shown) the second row 4 pin-holes, the third row 3 pin-holes, the fourth row 2 pin-holes.
The row marked with arrows is the last row before turning the corner.
Fix your pattern to the pillow as before. Wind ten pairs of bobbins with thread about the same thickness as 40 crochet cotton. Have enough coarse pins to keep three repeats of the pattern pinned to the pillow at all times.

Setting in and working the pattern

The Fan

Put a pin in hole No. 1. Remember the pin must lean slightly backwards. Hang four pairs of bobbins on to this pin. The pair on the outside left will be the 'workers'. This means they will follow the zig-zag marks on the pattern, making a stitch with the other pairs of bobbins as they go. The other three pairs are called 'passives'. They will stay on the outside edge of the Fan, all the time. Make a Full stitch with the workers and the first pair of passives. Twist both pairs once, right over left. Always twist right over left, otherwise the first part of your next stitch will undo the twist. Leave the first pair of passives on the left. Do a Full stitch with the workers and the second pair of passives. Twist both pairs once. Leave the second pair of passives on the left and do a Full stitch with the workers and the third pair of passives. Twist both pairs once.

Put a pin in hole No. 2 and hang a new pair of bobbins on to it. Work a Full stitch and twist with the workers and the new pair. Remove the pin from hole No. 2 and put it back in the same hole with the stitch just worked behind it. The new pair will be on the left of the pin and the workers on the right. Give the workers an extra twist. Always give the workers an extra twist when they are going round a pin.

Now work back to the left: Full stitch and twist the workers with the pair from No. 2 and then the three passives in turn. Give the workers an extra twist and put a pin in hole No. 3 with the workers behind it. The workers will be on the left of pin No. 3 and the passives on the right.

Full stitch and twist the workers with the three pairs of passives in turn, then with the pair from No. 2.

Put a pin in at hole No. 4 and hang on a new pair of bobbins. Full stitch and twist the workers with this new pair of bobbins, remove the pin and replace it in hole No. 4 with the stitch just worked behind it. Give the workers an extra twist. The new pair is on the left of the pin and the workers on the right.

Work back to the left: Full stitch and twist the workers with the pair from No. 4 then the pair from No. 2, then the three pairs of passives in turn. Give the workers an extra twist. Put a pin in hole No. 5 with the workers behind it. The workers will be on the left of pin No. 5 and the passives on the right.

Full stitch and twist the workers with the three pairs of passives, then the pairs from Nos 2 and 4. Put a pin in No. 6 and hang a new pair on it. Full stitch and twist the workers with this new pair. Remove the pin and replace it in No. 6 with the stitch just worked behind it. Give the workers an extra twist. The new pair is on the left of the pin and the workers are on the right.

Work back to the left: Full stitch and twist the workers with the new pair from No. 6, then with the pairs from Nos 4 and 2 and follow with the three pairs of passives in turn. Twist the workers once more and put a pin in hole No. 7. The workers will be on the left of pin No. 7 and the passives on the right.

Full stitch and twist the workers with the three pairs of passives in turn and the pairs from Nos 2, 4 and 6. Put a pin in at hole No. 8 and hang a new pair on it. Full stitch and twist the workers with the new pair. Remove the pin and replace it in No. 8 with the stitch just worked behind it. Give the workers an extra twist. The new pair is on the left of the pin and the workers on the right. Work back to the left: Full stitch and twist the workers with the pairs from Nos 8, 6, 4 and 2 and then the three passives. Give the workers an extra twist and put a pin in at hole No. 9 with the workers behind it. The workers are on the left of No. 9 and the passives on the right.

All the pairs for the Fan are now hung on. To complete the Fan we must now leave out pairs.

Full stitch and twist the workers with the three passives and the pairs from Nos 2, 4 and 6. Put a pin in at hole No. 10 with the workers behind it, then work back through the pairs from Nos 6, 4 and 2 and the passives and put in a pin at hole No. 11 with the workers behind it. Leave a pair out at No. 8. Did you remember to give the workers an extra twist round the pin?

Full stitch and twist the workers with the three passives and the pairs from Nos 2 and 4. Put in a pin at hole No. 12, then work back through the pairs from Nos 4 and 2 and the passives. Put in a pin at hole No. 13. Leave a pair out at No. 10.

Full stitch and twist the workers with the passives and the pair from No. 2. Put in a pin at hole No. 14. Work back through the pair from No. 2 and the passives. Put in a pin at hole No. 15. Leave a pair out at Nos 12 and 14. This is the end of the Fan.

Leave the workers (which should be on the left of the pin at hole No. 15) and the three pairs of passives on the left side of the pillow while the Ground is worked.

Twist the pairs left at Nos 8, 10, 12 and 14 once more before taking them into the Ground.

The Ground

The Ground work of this pattern consists of four rows of Torchon Ground, worked as in the first pattern.

Row 1. Put a pin in hole No. 16 and hang on a new pair of bobbins. Take the pair from No. 8 and the new pair from No. 16 and work a Full stitch. Remove the pin from No. 16 and replace it with the stitch just made, behind the pin. Work a Full stitch to cover the pin with the same two pairs. Twist both pairs twice. With the pair on the left of No. 16 and the pair from No. 10 work a Full stitch, pin, Full stitch and twist twice in hole No. 17.

Leave the right hand pair. With the pair from the left of No. 17 and the pair from No. 12 work Full stitch, pin, Full stitch and twist twice into hole No. 18. Leave the right hand pair. With the left hand pair from No. 18 and the pair from No. 14 work Full stitch, pin, Full stitch and twist twice into hole No. 19.

Row 2. Move all the bobbins back to the left of the pillow. Put a pin in hole No. 20 and hang on it the last pair of bobbins. Using this pair and the pair from No. 16 work a Full stitch. Remove the pin and replace it in hole No. 20 with the stitch just made behind it. Work another Full stitch to cover the pin with these two pairs and twist them both twice. Complete this row of Ground by joining the pairs from Nos 17 and 20 at No. 21; the pairs from Nos 18 and 21 at No. 22 and the pairs from Nos 19 and 22 at No. 23.

Row 3. Move the bobbins over to the left and work the next row, joining the pairs from Nos 20 and 21 at No. 24; the pairs from Nos 22 and 24 at No. 25 and the pairs from Nos 23 and 25 at No. 26.

Row 4. Move the bobbins over to the left of the pillow and work the last row of Ground. Join the pairs from Nos 24 and 25 at No. 27 and the pairs from Nos 26 and 27 at No. 28.
This completes the Ground. The pairs left hanging at Nos 19, 23, 26 and 28 will be picked up in the next Fan.

To continue

The second Fan

Remember to give the workers an extra twist when they go round a pin.
Bring back the workers and the passives at hole No. 15 which is hole No. 1 of this Fan.
Full stitch and twist 4 pairs to the right using 3 passives and the pair from No. 19. Pin in hole No. 2. Work back: Full stitch and twist 4 pairs left. Pin in hole No. 3.

Full stitch and twist 5 pairs to the right using 3 passives and the pairs from Nos 19 and 23. Pin in hole No. 4. Work back: Full stitch and twist 5 pairs left. Pin in hole No. 5.

Full stitch and twist 6 pairs right, using 3 passives and the pairs from Nos 19, 23 and 26. Pin in hole No. 6. Work back: Full stitch and twist 6 pairs left. Pin in hole No. 7.

Full stitch and twist 7 pairs to the right, using 3 passives and the pairs from Nos 19, 23, 26 and 28. Pin in hole No. 8. Work back: Full stitch and twist 7 pairs left. Pin in hole No. 9.

To complete the Fan we must now leave out pairs.
Full stitch and twist 6 pairs to the right. Pin in hole No. 10. Work back: Full stitch and twist 6 pairs left. Pin in hole No. 11. Leave a pair out at No. 8.
Full stitch and twist 5 pairs to the right. Pin in hole No. 12. Work back: Full stitch and twist 5 pairs left. Pin in hole No. 13. Leave a pair out at No. 10.
Full stitch and twist 4 pairs to the right. Pin in hold No. 14. Work back: Full stitch and twist 4 pairs left. Pin in hole No. 15. Leave a pair out at No. 12 and No. 14.

Leave the workers and the passives on the left; a pair from No. 14 will also go into the next Ground.

The second Ground

Move the bobbins over to the left of the pillow and begin to work the 4 rows of Ground from the right hand side, with Full stitch, pin, Full stitch and twist twice at each pin-hole.

Remember the pairs from Nos 8, 10, 12 and 14 need to be twisted twice before using them in the Ground.

    Row 1: Work holes Nos 16 to 20.
    Row 2: Work holes Nos 21 to 24.
    Row 3: Work holes Nos 25 to 27.
    Row 4: Work holes Nos 28 to 29.

Continue working the Fan and Ground alternately until the corner is reached.

The corner

When the last Fan before the corner is complete, take the workers and the first pair of passives and work a Full stitch to cover the last pin. Twist both pairs twice.

Work another Full stitch with the same two pairs and put a pin between them, in the first hole of the Fan round the corner.

Turn the pillow round and the bobbins will be in position to make the next Fan. Make this Fan but give an extra twist to the pairs you take in, before picking them up.

When the Fan is complete do the Ground. The first two rows of Ground will have the same number of pin-holes as the two rows at the **very** beginning, that is Nos 16 to 19 and 20 to 23.

To set up

Follow the same instructions as for setting up the first pattern (p.13), fitting the first Fan after the corner to the first Fan of the pattern.

To finish off

Work as for turning the corner, but instead of working the next Fan, work across the passives and the first pair to be picked up at hole No. 2. Work a Full stitch to cover the pin with the workers and the pair picked up. Leave the workers.

Using the pair picked up, work a row of Ground stitches across the pattern, from left to right, using holes Nos 4, 6, 8, 16 and 20. This row will overlap with the very first row.

Tie the threads and cut off the bobbins. Join neatly, darn in the ends and mount.

Variations

To make a change, the Fan part of this pattern can be worked in Cloth stitch. A series of Full stitches without any twists makes a piece of fabric similar to simple woven cloth — and this is what we call Cloth stitch. So just leave out the twists between the stitches and only twist the workers at the pins. Another change is to work in Cloth stitch but to twist the workers three times between the passives and the other pairs, making a ladder effect along the edge.

POINTS TO REMEMBER

Always twist right over left, otherwise the next stitch will undo the twist.
Always give the workers an extra twist when they are going round a pin.
Watch the distance between the pin-holes, and make sure the threads are well twisted between them. If your thread is a little finer put in an extra twist. If it is a little coarser then leave out a twist. Two twists are needed between holes when working the Torchon Ground in this book with 40 crochet cotton.
Always pull your work up tightly to the pin.
Whilst working hold your hands as if you were playing the piano and not as if you were holding a cup and saucer, so that when making the stitches the bobbins are moving on the pillow and not in the air.
Remember that all pins should lean slightly backwards and the ones on the outside edges should also lean slightly outwards.
Watch the threads whilst working NOT the bobbins.
To prevent the lace becoming soiled handle the thread as little as possible, and keep the finished parts of the lace covered up until the whole is complete.
To make your lace longer than the pattern simply set up before turning the corner but you MUST have at least two complete repeats of the pattern pinned down to the pricking before you undo the bundle.

THIRD PATTERN

Prepare the pattern.

This pattern consists of a Cloth stitch footside and a Torchon or 'Dragon's Head' Fan. Cloth stitch is made by working a series of full stitches without any twists between them. The footside is the straight edge of the lace. The Torchon Fan is really the simple Fan turned sides to middle, but looking at it on the pillow, a dragon's head can be seen, with three 'teeth' on each 'jaw' and a long 'tongue' up the middle.

In this pattern we learn to make a firm straight edge to our lace, which will not draw up. This is done by using two pairs of workers on the footside, which work alternate rows.

Wind eight pairs of bobbins; three pairs will be workers. You need thread about the thickness of 40 crochet cotton. Have enough coarse pins to keep three repeats of the pattern pinned up. One complete repeat of a pattern is called a 'head'. Remember to keep your stitches pulled up tightly to the pins.

The footside

Hang two pairs of workers on the pin at hole No. 1. The first pair you hang on, keep to the left, the second pair to the right, otherwise the stitch slips undone when you take the pin out. Work a Full stitch with them. Remove the pin and replace it in hole No. 1, with the stitch just worked behind it. Work another Full stitch to cover the pin. Twist both pairs of workers twice. Note: only the workers are twisted in this footside, and then only at a pin. Hang a new pair of bobbins on a pin at hole No. 2. With the left hand pair of workers from hole No. 1 work a Full stitch with the pair at hole No. 2. Remove the pin and replace it in hole No. 2, with the stitch just made behind the pin. Twist the workers twice. Work a Full stitch with the workers and the pair from No. 2. Twist the workers twice.

Put a pin in hole No. 3, with the workers behind it. Now using the workers that have just been working and the pair of workers from the right which have been resting a row, make a Full stitch on the outside of the pin at No. 3. Twist both pairs twice. This will cause the workers to change places. The pair that has just been working will be left over on the right side and the pair that has been resting will be on the left side, waiting to work the next row. With the left hand pair of workers, work a Full stitch with the pair hanging from hole No. 2. Hang a new pair on a pin at hole No. 4. Work this pair with the workers. Remove the pin at No. 4 and replace it, with the new stitch behind it. Twist the workers twice. Work a Full stitch with the workers and the pairs from Nos 4 and 2. Twist the workers twice.

Put a pin in at hole No. 5, with the workers behind it. Work a Full stitch with the two pairs of workers, on the outside of the pin. Twist both pairs twice. Leave the pair on the right to rest. With the left hand pair of workers work Full stitches with the pairs from Nos 2 and 4. Hang a new pair on a pin at hole No. 6. Work a Full stitch with this pair and the workers. Remove the pin and replace in No. 6, with the stitch behind it. Twist the workers twice then work Full stitches with the workers and the pairs from Nos 6, 4 and 2 in turn. Twist the workers twice.

Put a pin in at hole No. 7, with the workers behind it. Work a Full stitch with the two pairs of workers, on the outside of the pin. Twist both pairs twice. Leave the right hand pair to rest and work the next row with the left hand pair. Work a Full stitch with the workers and the pairs from Nos 2, 4 and 6. Hang a new pair on a pin at hole No. 8. Work a Full stitch with this pair and the workers. Remove the pin and replace it in hole No. 8, with the stitch just made behind the pin. Twist the workers twice. Work a Full stitch with the workers and the pairs from Nos 8, 6, 4 and 2 in turn. Twist the workers twice.

Put a pin in at hole No. 9, with the workers behind it. Work a Full stitch with the two pairs of workers, on the outside of the pin. Twist both pairs twice. The bobbins for the footside are now all on. Complete the footside by working it in Full stitch, changing the workers for each row and leaving out one pair at pins Nos 8, 10, 12 and 14, thus:

From No. 9 work three pairs: Nos 2, 4 and 6, across to hole No. 10. Leave out a pair at hole No. 8. Work back to hole No. 11.

From No. 11 work two pairs: Nos 2 and 4, across to hole No. 12. Leave out a pair at hole No. 10. Work back to hole No. 13.

From No. 13 work one pair: No. 2, across to hole No. 14. Leave out a pair at hole No. 12. Work back to hole No. 15.

The pairs from Nos 8, 10, 12 and 14 will be picked up in the next Fan. Leave the two pairs of workers on the outside of the pin at hole No. 15 and work the Fan.

The Fan

Put a pin in hole No. 16 and hang two pairs of bobbins on it. Remember to keep the first pair to the left. Work a Full stitch. Remove the pin and replace it in hole No. 16, with the stitch just made behind it. The pair of bobbins on the left of the pin will be the workers for the Fan. The Fan is worked in Full stitch and twist once, but remember to give the workers an extra twist at the pins.

Twist the pairs from Nos 8, 10, 12 and 14 twice before taking them into the Fan.

Work the Fan with the workers on the left of the pin No. 16 as follows:

Full stitch and twist four pairs from Nos 16, 8, 10 and 12. Pin at No. 17. Work back to No. 18 and pin.
Full stitch and twist three pairs from Nos 18, 8 and 10. Pin at No. 19. Work back to No. 20 and pin.
Full stitch and twist two pairs from Nos 20 and 8. Pin at No. 21. Work back to No. 22 and pin.
Full stitch and twist five pairs from Nos 22, 21, 19, 17 and 14. Pin at No. 23. Work back to No. 24 and pin.
Full stitch and twist two pairs from Nos 24 and 21. Pin at No. 25. Work back to No. 26 and pin.
Full stitch and twist three pairs from Nos 26, 25 and 19. Pin at No. 27. Work back to No. 28 and pin.
Full stitch and twist four pairs from Nos 28, 25, 27 and 17. Pin at No. 29. Work back to No. 30 and pin.

This completes the Fan. Leave the workers on the left of pin No. 30 and the pair of passives on the right. These two pairs only come into the Fan. The pairs from holes Nos 25, 27, 29 and 23, all need to be twisted twice in readiness to be worked across into the next footside.

Hole No. 15 of the first footside is also hole No. 1 of the next footside.

The second footside

Work the next footside as follows: with the left hand pair of workers resting at hole No. 15 (now hole No. 1) and the pair from No. 23 make a Full stitch. Twist the workers twice and put a pin in at hole No. 2, with the stitch just made behind it. Work a Full stitch with the workers and the pair from No. 23 again. Twist the workers twice.

Put a pin in at hole No. 3, with the workers behind it. Work a Full stitch with the two pairs of workers, on the outside of the pin. Twist both pairs twice. Using the left hand pair of workers, make a Full stitch with the pairs from

Nos 2 and 29. Twist the workers twice. Put a pin in at hole No. 4, with the stitch just made behind it. Work a Full stitch with the workers and the pairs from Nos 29 and 2. Twist the workers twice.

Put a pin in at hole No. 5, with the workers behind it. Work a Full stitch with the two pairs of workers, on the outside of the pin. Twist both pairs twice. Using the left hand pair of workers, make Full stitches with the pairs from Nos 2, 4 and 27. Twist the workers twice. Put a pin in hole No. 6, with the stitch just made behind it. Make Full stitches with the workers and the pairs from Nos 27, 4 and 2. Twist the workers twice.

Put a pin in at hole No. 7, with the workers behind it. Work a Full stitch with the two pairs of workers, on the outside of the pin. Twist both pairs twice. Using the left hand pair of workers make Full stitches with the pairs from Nos 2, 4, 6 and 25. Twist the workers twice. Put a pin in at hole No. 8, with the stitch just made behind it. Make Full stitches with the workers and the pairs from Nos 25, 6, 4 and 2. Twist the workers twice.

Put a pin in at hole No. 9, with the workers behind it. Work a Full stitch with the two pairs of workers, on the outside of the pin. Twist both pairs twice. Now begin to leave out pairs to be picked up in the next Fan. Remember that the pairs left out need to be twisted twice before being taken into the Fan.

To continue

Work in the same manner, but reduce the number of stitches in each row by one.
From No. 9 work three pairs: Nos 2, 4 and 6, across to hole No. 10. Leave out a pair at No. 8. Work back to hole No. 11.
From No. 11 work two pairs: Nos 2 and 4, across to hole No. 12. Leave out a pair at No. 10. Work back to hole No. 13.
From hole No. 13 work one pair: No. 2, across to hole No. 14. Leave out a pair at No. 12. Work back to hole No. 15.
The pairs from Nos 8, 10, 12 and 14 will be picked up in the next Fan. Leave the two pairs of workers on the outside of pin No. 15 and work the next Fan.

The second Fan

Using the workers on the left of pin No. 30 make the next Fan. Remember to give the workers an extra twist at the pins.
Full stitch and twist 4 pairs, pin. Work back 4 pairs, pin.
Full stitch and twist 3 pairs, pin. Work back 3 pairs, pin.
Full stitch and twist 2 pairs, pin. Work back 2 pairs, pin.
Full stitch and twist 5 pairs, pin. Work back 5 pairs, pin.
Full stitch and twist 2 pairs, pin. Work back 2 pairs, pin.
Full stitch and twist 3 pairs, pin. Work back 3 pairs, pin.
Full stitch and twist 4 pairs, pin. Work back 4 pairs, pin.
This completes the second Fan. Leave the workers on the left of pin No. 16 and the passives on the right of pin No. 16. They only come into the Fan. Twist the pairs from Nos 25, 27, 29 and 23 twice, in readiness to be worked across into the next footside.

The corner

When the corner is reached it will be noticed that one pin-hole from the outside edge of the footside is missing: pin-hole No. 15. This means that the workers and the pair to be left at hole No. 14 will both be left at pin-hole No. 14. Neither pair of workers will be used again until after the corner has been turned. The corner is simple. Make two Fans, one after the other following the number order on the working diagram. This will mean:

a. Full stitch and twist 4 pairs to No. 17, pin. Work back to No. 18 and pin.
   Full stitch and twist 3 pairs to No. 19, pin. Work back to No. 20 and pin.
   Full stitch and twist 2 pairs to No. 21, pin. Work back to No. 22 and pin.
   Full stitch and twist 5 pairs to No. 23, pin. Work back to No. 24 and pin.
   Full stitch and twist 2 pairs to No. 25, pin. Work back to No. 26 and pin.
   Full stitch and twist 3 pairs to No. 27, pin. Work back to No. 28 and pin.
   Full stitch and twist 4 pairs to No. 29, pin. Work back to No. 30 and pin.

b. Full stitch and twist 4 pairs to No. 31, pin. Work back to No. 32 and spin.
   Full stitch and twist 3 pairs to No. 33, pin. Work back to No. 34 and pin.
   Full stitch and twist 2 pairs to No. 35, pin. Work back to No. 36 and pin.
   Full stitch and twist 5 pairs to No. 37, pin. Work back to No. 38 and pin.
   Full stitch and twist 2 pairs to No. 39, pin. Work back to No. 40 and pin.
   Full stitch and twist 3 pairs to No. 41, pin. Work back to No. 42 and pin.
   Full stitch and twist 4 pairs to No. 43, pin. Work back to No. 44 and pin.

Take the pair from hole No. 37 (the top of the second Fan) and twist twice. Using this pair and the workers left at hole No. 14 work a Full stitch. Twist the workers twice. Put a pin in at No. 2. Work a Full stitch again to cover the pin. Twist the workers twice. Put a pin in at No. 3, with the workers behind it.

Work a Full stitch with both pairs of workers on the outside of the pin.

Continue working the footside as before.

Continue working until four corners have been turned. Work an overlap row in Torchon Ground using holes Nos 1, 2, 4, 6 and 8.

Join neatly and mount.

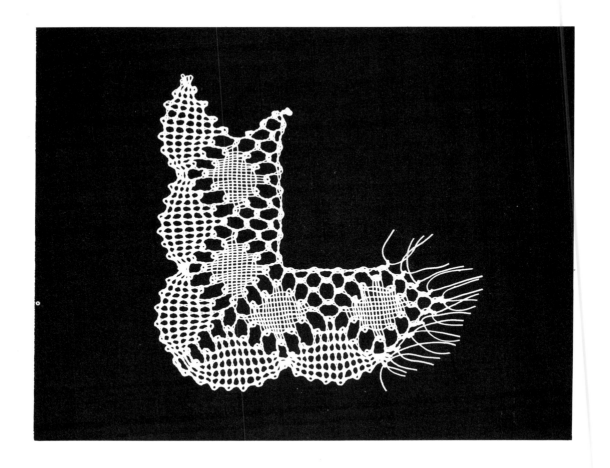

FOURTH PATTERN

Prepare the pattern as before, by pricking it on to card and inking it in.
This pattern consists of a simple Fan, as in the second pattern, a Torchon
Ground also as in the second pattern, and a Cloth stitch Bud: a diamond
shaped block of Cloth stitch in the middle of the lace.
Wind thirteen pairs of bobbins with thread about the thickness of 40 crochet cotton. Have enough coarse pins to keep three repeats of the pattern, or three
'heads', pinned to the pillow at all times.

Setting in and working the pattern

The Fan

The Fan is set in and made in exactly the same way as the one in the second
pattern. Remember that when you hang on a new pair of bobbins, you put a
pin in the hole where the new pair is required and hang the new pair on the
pin. Work the new pair with the workers, take out the pin and replace it in

the same hole, with the stitch just made, behind the pin. Make another stitch with the new pair and the workers.

Put a pin in hole No. 1. Hang 4 pairs of bobbins on it. The pair on the outside left will be the workers. Make a Full stitch with the workers and the 3 pairs of passives in turn. Hang a new pair on a pin at hole No. 2. Work back: Full stitch and twist 4 pairs left. Pin in hole No. 3.

Full stitch and twist 4 pairs to the right. Hang a new pair on pin No. 4. Work back: Full stitch and twist 5 pairs left. Pin in hole No. 5.

Full stitch and twist 5 pairs to the right. Hang a new pair on a pin at hole No. 6. Work back: Full stitch and twist 6 pairs left. Pin in hole No. 7.

Full stitch and twist 6 pairs to the right. Hang a new pair on a pin at hole No. 8. Work back: Full stitch and twist 7 pairs left. Pin in hole No. 9.

Now we begin to leave pairs out to go into the Bud.
Full stitch and twist 6 pairs to the right to hole No. 10. Work back: Full stitch and twist 6 pairs to hole No. 11, leaving a pair out at hole No. 8.

Full stitch and twist 5 pairs to the right to hole No. 12. Work back: Full stitch and twist 5 pairs to hole No. 13, leaving a pair out at hole No. 10.

Full stitch and twist 4 pairs to the right to hole No. 14. Work back: Full stitch and twist 4 pairs to hole No. 15, leaving a pair out at holes Nos 12 and 14.

Leave the workers and the 3 pairs of passives on the left. The pairs left out at holes Nos 8, 10, 12 and 14 will be taken into the Bud later. Remember to twist them twice before they are taken into the Bud.

The Ground

This is Torchon Ground and is made by Full stitch, pin, Full stitch twist twice, at each hole. It consists of 4 rows worked from right to left following the same principle as in the second pattern.

Row 1. Begin by hanging 2 pairs of bobbins on a pin at hole No. 16. Keep the first pair to the left. Make a stitch, take out the pin and replace it in hole No. 16 with the stitch just made behind the pin. Make another stitch and twist twice. This leaves two pairs hanging on pin No. 16. Hang a new pair on a pin at hole No. 17. With the left hand pair from No. 16 and the new pair at No. 17 make a Full stitch at No. 17. Take out the pin and replace in No. 17 with the stitch just made behind it. Make another stitch and twist twice. Now there are two pairs of bobbins on the pin at hole No. 17. Hang a new pair on a pin at hole No. 18. With the left hand pair from No. 17 and the new pair from No. 18 make. a Full stitch at No. 18. Take out the pin and replace in No. 18 with the stitch just made behind it. Make another stitch and twist twice. This leaves two pairs hanging on pin No. 18. Hang a new pair on a pin at hold No. 19. With the left hand pair from No. 18 and the new pair from No. 19 make a Full stitch at No. 19. Take out the pin and replace in No. 19 with the stitch just made behind it. Make another stitch and twist twice. There will be two pairs hanging on pin No. 19. The left hand pair of these will eventually join with the pair from the top of the Fan (No. 8) to start the Bud at hole No. 26. But we must complete the Ground first.

Go back to the right and work the remaining 3 rows:

    Row 2: Work holes Nos 20 to 22.

    Row 3: Work holes Nos 23, 24.

    Row 4: Work hole No. 25.

The Bud

This is made in Cloth stitch which means that the workers will make Full stitches with all the other pairs in turn, but there will be no twisting, except when the workers are going round the pin and then they will be twisted twice. In other words, at the end of each row, twist the workers twice.

Take the pair left out at No. 8 and the pair left at No. 19. Work a Full stitch, pin, Full stitch with them in hole No. 26. The left hand pair of these two will be the workers for the Bud; the other pair will run straight down the centre of the Bud (to hole No. 37).

With the workers, pick up the pair left at No. 10. 'Pick up' means work a Full stitch with the workers and the pair from No. 10, to bring the pair from No. 10 into the Bud. Twist the workers twice, put a pin in at hole No. 27. Work back 2 Full stitches with the pairs from Nos 27 and 26.

Pick up the pair left at No. 22. Twist the workers twice, put a pin in at hole No. 28. Work 3 Full stitches with the pairs from Nos 28, 26 and 27.

Pick up the pair left at No. 12. Twist the workers twice and put a pin in at hole No. 29. Work back 4 full stitches with the pairs from Nos 29, 27, 26 and 28.

Pick up the pair left at No. 24. Twist the workers twice and put a pin in at hole No. 30. Work 5 Full stitches with the pairs from Nos 30, 28, 26, 27 and 29.

Pick up the pair left at No. 14. Twist the workers twice and put a pin in at hole No. 31. Work back 6 Full stitches with the pairs from Nos 31, 29, 27, 26, 28 and 30.

Pick up the pair left at hole No. 25. Twist the workers twice and put a pin in at hole No. 32.

Now we must leave out pairs to shape the lower part of the Bud.

Work 6 Full stitches with the pairs from Nos 32, 30, 28, 26, 27 and 29. Twist the workers twice and put a pin in at hole No. 33, leaving a pair out at No. 31. Work back 5 Full stitches with the pairs from Nos 33, 27, 26, 28 and 30. Twist the workers twice and put in a pin at hole No. 34, leaving out a pair at No. 32.

Work 4 Full stitches with the pairs from Nos 34, 28, 26 and 27. Twist the workers twice and put a pin in at hole No. 35, leaving out a pair at No. 33. Work back 3 Full stitches with the pairs from Nos 35, 26 and 28. Twist the workers twice and put a pin in at hole No. 36, leaving a pair out at hole No. 34.

WORK CARDS

WORK CARD

PRICKING

number
of pairs
per
pin

1
1
1
1
2

WORKING DIAGRAM

START 1
2
3 6
4 7
5 8 11
9 12
10 13
14
15

TURN PILLOW

11
7 16
4 12 17
8 13 18
9 14 19
1 2 3 5 6 10 15 20

CORNER

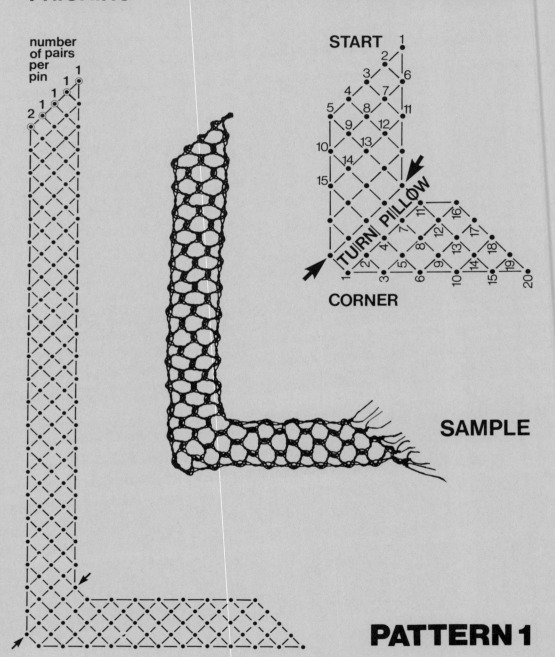

SAMPLE

PATTERN 1

WORK CARD

2

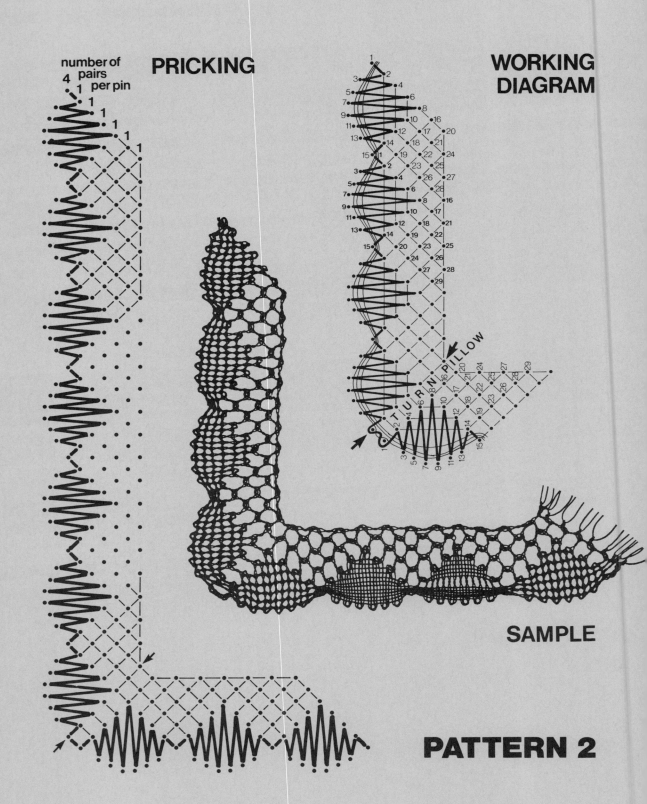

PRICKING

number of pairs per pin
4
1
1
1
1
1
1
1

WORKING DIAGRAM

SAMPLE

PATTERN 2

WORK CARD

3

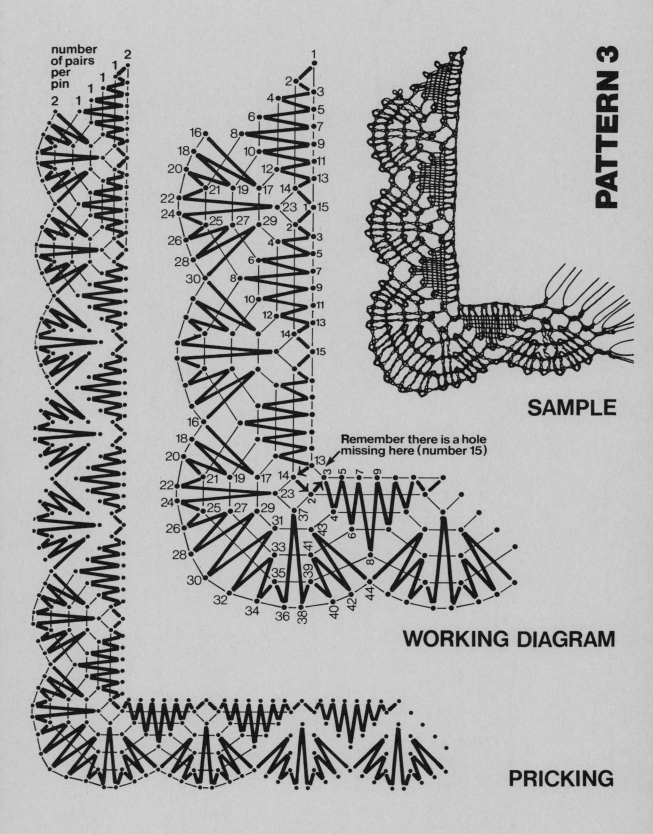

number of pairs per pin

2   1   1   1 1 2

PATTERN 3

SAMPLE

Remember there is a hole missing here (number 15)

WORKING DIAGRAM

PRICKING

WORK CARD

4

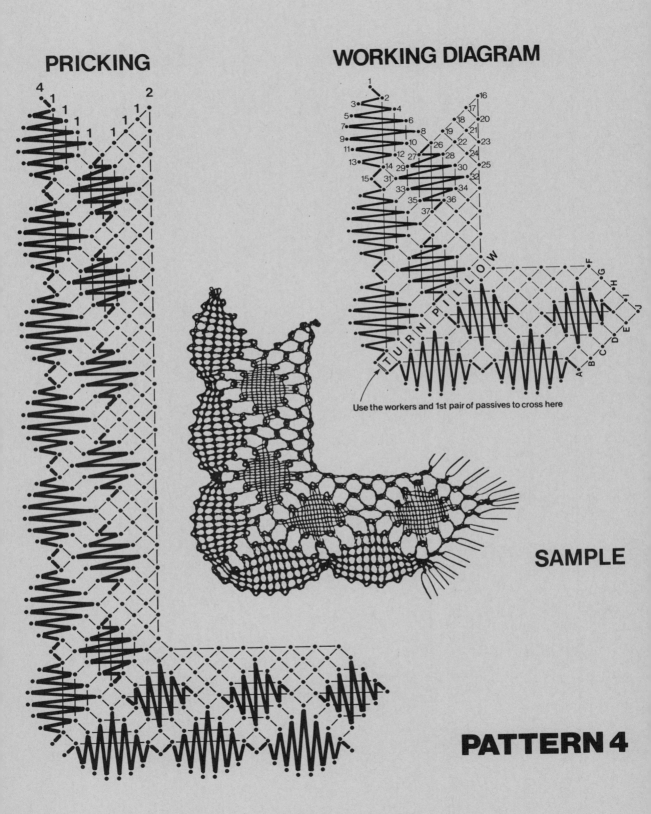

PRICKING

WORKING DIAGRAM

Use the workers and 1st pair of passives to cross here

TURN PILLOW

SAMPLE

PATTERN 4

WORK CARD
5

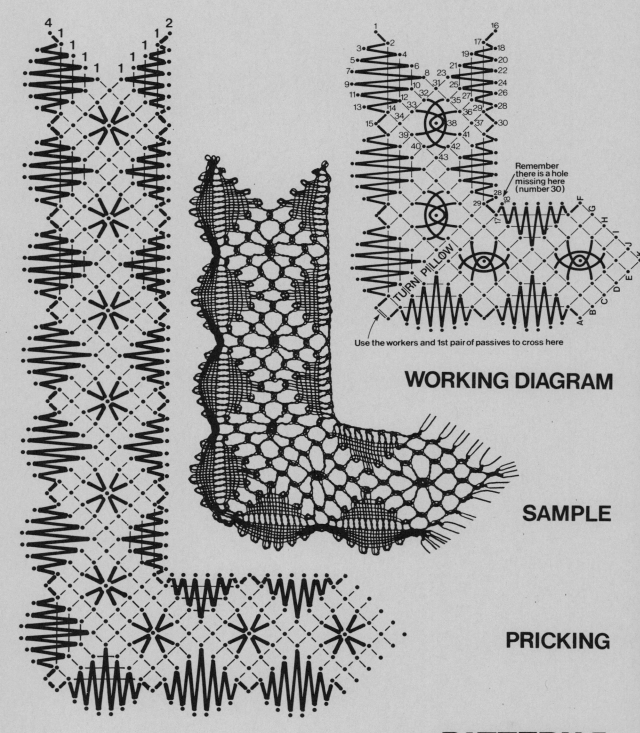

WORKING DIAGRAM

Remember there is a hole missing here (number 30)

Use the workers and 1st pair of passives to cross here

TURN PILLOW

SAMPLE

PRICKING

PATTERN 5

WORK CARD

PATTERN 6

PRICKING

SAMPLE

WORKING DIAGRAM

Work 2 Full stitches with the pairs from Nos 36 and 26. Twist the workers twice and put a pin in at hole No. 37. Work one Full stitch to cover pin No. 37, leaving a pair out at hole No. 36, and two pairs on No. 37. Twist all the pairs coming from the Bud twice. They are now ready to be worked into the next Fan or Ground, depending on which side they are. The left hand pair on pin No. 37 will go into the next Fan. The right hand pair will go into the Ground. Continue working the parts of the pattern in turn, Fan, Ground, Bud, until the corner is reached.

The corner

As in the other corners, part of the Ground is missing. When turning corners in lace, you will always have to work extra sections on the outside of the lace. In Torchon lace this usually means making two Fans, one after the other. Complete the Fan immediately before the corner. This will mean that the lace made so far makes a diagonal edge across the pattern.
With the workers from the Fan and the first pair of passives, make a Full stitch to cover the last pin in the Fan. Twist both pairs twice, and make another stitch with them. Turn the pillow and put a pin in the first hole of the next Fan, with the workers on the left of it and the passives on the right. The bobbins are now in place to make the next Fan, but remember to twist all the pairs twice as they come across the corner. Make the next Fan, then make the next Bud. Use the pairs left out from the first Fan after the corner and those from the last Bud before the corner, to make the next Bud. Make another Fan, then go across and make the Ground.
When you have turned four corners make an overlap row, working Ground stitches to fit the beginning of your lace. Use the edge of a Fan and a row of Ground as indicated by the letters A to E and F to J.

FIFTH PATTERN

Prepare the pattern as before, by pricking it on to card and inking it in.
This pattern consists of a simple Fan worked in Cloth stitch with a ladder, a
Cloth stitch footside as in the third pattern and a Spider. Cloth stitch means
no twisting except the workers when they go round a pin. To make the ladder,
twist the workers twice between the passives and the other pairs
Wind fourteen pairs of bobbins with thread the thickness of 40 crochet cotton.
Have enough coarse pins to keep three 'heads' (or repeats of the pattern) pinned
to the pillow at all times.

Setting in and working the pattern

The Fan

Set in the Fan and work it as follows: Put a pin in hole No. 1. Hang 4 pairs
of bobbins on it. The pair on the outside left will be the workers. Full stitch
with the workers and the 3 pairs of passives in turn. Twist the workers twice.

Put a pin in hole No. 2. Hang a new pair of bobbins on it. Work a Full stitch. Twist the workers only twice. Remove the pin and replace in hole No. 2, with the stitch just made behind it.

Work back to the left. Full stitch with the workers and the pair from No. 2. Twist the workers only twice. Full stitch the workers and the 3 pairs of passives in turn. Twist the workers only twice. Put a pin in at hole No. 3, with the workers behind it.

Full stitch with the workers and the 3 pairs of passives in turn. Twist the workers only twice. Full stitch the workers and the pair from No. 2. Put a pin in at hole No. 4 and hang a new pair on it. Work a Full stitch with the workers and the new pair. Twist the workers only twice. Remove the pin and replace in hole No. 4 with the stitch just made behind it.

Work back to the left. Full stitch with the workers and the pairs from Nos 4 and 2. Twist the workers only twice. Full stitch the workers and the 3 pairs of passives in turn. Twist the workers only twice. Put a pin in hole No. 5 with the workers behind it.

Full stitch the workers with the 3 pairs of passives in turn. Twist the workers only twice. Full stitch the workers with the pairs from Nos 2 and 4. Put a pin in at hole No. 6. Hang a new pair on it. Full stitch the workers and the new pair. Twist the workers only twice. Remove the pin and replace it in No. 6, with the stitch just made behind it.

Work back to the left. Full stitch the workers and the pairs from Nos 6, 4 and 2. Twist the workers only twice. Full stitch the workers and the 3 pairs of passives in turn. Twist the workers only twice. Put a pin in at hole No. 7, with the workers behind it.

Full stitch the workers with the 3 pairs of passives in turn. Twist the workers only twice. Full stitch the workers and the pairs from Nos 2, 4 and 6. Put a pin in at hole No. 8. Hang a new pair on it. Full stitch the workers and the new pair. Twist the workers only twice. Remove the pin and replace in No. 8, with the stitch just made behind it.

Work back to the left. Full stitch the workers and the pairs from Nos 8, 6, 4 and 2. Twist the workers only twice. Full stitch the workers with the 3 pairs of passives in turn. Twist the workers only twice. Put a pin in at hole No. 9, with the workers behind it.

All the pairs from the Fan are now hung on. To complete the Fan continue working in this manner, leaving out pairs at Nos 8, 10, 12 and 14. These pairs will go into the Spider.

The Footside

Hang two pairs of workers on the pin at hole No. 16. The first pair you hang on keep to the left, the second pair to the right, otherwise the stitch slips undone when you take the pin out. Work a Full stitch with them. Remove the pin and replace in hole No. 16, with the stitch just made behind it. Work another Full stitch to cover the pin. Twist both pairs of workers twice. Hang a new pair of bobbins on a pin at hole No. 17. With the left hand pair of workers make a Full stitch with the pair at hole No. 17. Remove the pin and replace it in No. 17, with the stitch just made behind the pin. Twist the workers twice.

Note: only the workers are twisted in this footside, and then only at a pin.

Put a pin in hole No. 18, with the workers behind it. Now using the workers that have just been working and the pair of workers from the right which have been resting a row, make a Full stitch on the outside of the pin at No. 18. Twist both pairs twice. This will cause the workers to change places. The pair that has just been working will be left over on the right side and the pair that has been resting will be on the left side, waiting to work the next row.

With the left hand pair of workers, make a Full stitch with the pair hanging from hole No. 17.

Hang a new pair on a pin at hole No. 19. Work this pair with the workers. Remove the pin at No. 19 and replace it, with the new stitch behind it. Twist the workers twice. Make a Full stitch with the workers and the pairs from Nos 19 and 17. Twist the workers twice.

Put a pin in at hole No. 20. Work a Full stitch with the two pairs of workers, on the outside of the pin. Twist both pairs twice. Leave the pair on the right to rest. With the left hand pair of workers make Full stitches with the pairs from Nos 17 and 19.

Hang a new pair on a pin at hole No. 21. Work a Full stitch with this pair and the workers. Remove the pin and replace in No. 21, with the stitch behind it. Twist the workers twice then make Full stitches with the workers and the pairs from Nos 21, 19 and 17 in turn. Twist the workers twice.

Put a pin in at hole No. 22, with the workers behind it. Make a Full stitch with the two pairs of workers, on the outside of the pin. Twist both pairs twice. Leave the right hand pair to rest and work the next row with the left hand pair. Work a Full stitch with the workers and the pairs from Nos 17, 19 and 21.

Hang a new pair on a pin at hole No. 23. Make a Full stitch with this pair and the workers. Remove the pin and replace it in hole No. 23, with the stitch just made behind the pin. Twist the workers twice. Work a Full stitch with the workers and the pairs from Nos 23, 21, 19 and 17 in turn. Twist the workers twice.

Put a pin in at hole No. 24, with the workers behind it. Make a Full stitch with the two pairs of workers, on the outside of the pin. Twist both pairs twice.

The bobbins for the footside are now all on. Complete the footside by continuing to work it in Full stitch, changing the workers for each row as before and leaving out pairs at Nos 23, 25, 27 and 29. These pairs will be picked up in the Spider. Twist all these pairs twice.

The Spider

Each Spider is 'fenced in' with a Full stitch Torchon ground; two sides before the Spider and 2 sides after.

Take the pair from No. 8 and the pair from No. 23. Make a Full stitch, put in the pin at hole No. 31, with the stitch just made behind it. Cover with a Full stitch. Twist both pairs twice.

With the left hand pair from No. 31 and the pair from No. 10, Full stitch, pin, Full stitch, twist twice, into hole No. 32.

With the left hand pair from No. 32 and the pair from No. 12, Full stitch, pin, Full stitch, twist twice, into hole No. 33.

With the left hand pair from No. 33 and the pair from No. 14, Full stitch, pin, Full stitch, twist twice, into hole No. 34.

Go back to hole No. 31. Take the pair still hanging there and the pair from No. 25, Full stitch, pin, Full stitch, twist, twice, into hole No. 35.

Take the right hand pair from No. 35 and the pair from No. 27, Full stitch, pin, Full stitch, twist twice, into hole No. 36.

Take the right hand pair from No. 36 and the pair from No. 29, Full stitch, pin, Full stitch, twist twice, into hole No. 37.

This completes the two sides of the 'fence' of the Spider before starting.

The pairs from Nos 33, 32, 35 and 36 will be the Spider's 'legs'. Twist them once more making 3 twists in all.

  With the 'leg' from No. 32, Full stitch the 'legs' from Nos 35 and 36.
  With the 'leg' from No. 33, Full stitch the 'legs' from Nos 35 and 36.

The 'legs' have now crossed over. Put in a pin at the centre, hole No. 38, so that the 'legs' from Nos 33 and 32 are on the right and the 'legs' from Nos 36 and 35 are on the left of the pin.

Now we must take the 'legs' back to their own side.

  With the 'leg' which originally came from No. 36, Full stitch the 'legs' which came from Nos 33 and 32.

  With the 'leg' which originally came from No. 35, Full stitch the 'legs' which came from Nos 33 and 32. Twist all 'legs' three times.

An easy way to remember how to make a Spider is:- Full stitch the middle two 'legs', then the right two, then the left two, then the middles again. Put in the pin, then middles, right, left, and finally the middles again and twist three times

Now we must complete the Spider's 'fence'.

With the right hand pair from No. 34 and the Spider's 'leg' from No. 33, Full stitch, pin, Full stitch, twist twice, into hole No. 39.

With the right hand pair from No. 39 and the 'leg' from No. 32, Full stitch, pin, Full stitch, twist twice, into hole No. 40.

With the left hand pair from No. 37, and the 'leg' from No. 36, Full stitch, pin, Full stitch, twist twice, into hole No. 41.

With the left hand pair from No. 41 and the 'leg' from No. 35, Full stitch, pin, Full stitch, twist twice, into hole No. 42.

With the left hand pair from No. 42 and the right hand pair from No. 40, Full stitch, pin, Full stitch, twist twice, into hole No. 43.

This completes the Spider's 'fence'. Continue working the pattern, to the corner.

The corner

The Fan turns the corner as in the second and fourth patterns. With the workers from the Fan and the first pair of passives, make a Full stitch to cover the last pin in the Fan. Twist both pairs twice, and make another stitch with them. Turn the pillow and put a pin in the first hole of the next Fan, with the workers on the left of it and the passives on the right. The bobbins are now in place to make the next Fan, but remember to twist all the pairs twice as they come across the corner.

Use the pairs left out from the first Fan after the corner and those from the last Spider before the corner, to make the next Spider.

The footside turns the corner as in the third pattern. Hole No. 30 will be missing. The workers will have to wait at hole No. 29 until the corner is complete. They will then work across to what will be hole No. 17 in the next footside, before reaching the footside edge again at No. 18.

Setting Up

Set up so that you have 7 Spiders between the corners.

When you have finished your lace, work an overlap row in Ground stitches using the holes along the edge of a Fan and a footside, as indicated by the letters A to E and F to K on the working diagram.

SIXTH PATTERN

Prepare the pattern as before but pin it on to the pillow so that this time the corner is at the top of the pillow.

This pattern consists of a Cloth stitch Trail, a Torchon Ground and a Torchon or Dragon's Head Fan.

The Cloth stitch Trail which runs down the centre of the pattern is really an elongated Cloth stitch Bud. It starts and ends in just the same way. In the main part of the Trail itself, you are either taking in pairs from the Ground and leaving pairs out for the Fan, or taking in pairs from the Fan and leaving out pairs for the Ground. At each turning point in the Trail, there is one hole where there is neither a pair picked up nor left out, eg Nos 9, 27. This is the point at which to leave the workers from the Trail to rest, while working either the Fan or Ground. When the Trail changes direction, so does the number of pairs of bobbins in it. When the Trail is working to the right, towards the footside, you will work across 4 pairs and pick up 1 pair - 5 pairs in all. When the Trail is moving to the left, towards the Fan, you will work across 5 pairs and pick up 1 pair — 6 pairs in all.

The Fan is slightly larger than the one in the third pattern; the Dragon has an extra tooth! The Ground is as in the second pattern.

The corner of the pattern is pinned at the top of the pillow which will make starting easier because the Trail narrows down to a point at the corner and by starting at the point, we are sure to get the correct number of bobbins for the Trail.

The holes marked with a ring (Nos 9, 27) **do not** have a pair of bobbins picked up from them, nor left out at them.

Wind fourteen pairs of bobbins with thread the thickness of 40 crochet cotton. Have enough coarse pins to hold three 'heads' pinned to the pillow at all times.

Setting in and working the pattern

The Trail

Hang two pairs of bobbins on a pin at hole No. 1. Remember to keep the first pair to the left. Make a Full stitch, remove the pin and replace in hole No. 1, with the stitch just made behind it. Make another Full stitch to cover the pin. The left hand pair of these two will be the workers for the Trail. Hang a new pair on pin No. 2. With the workers and the new pair make a Full stitch. Twist the workers twice, take out the pin and replace it with the workers behind it. With the workers make a Full stitch with the pair from No. 2 and the pair from No. 1. Hang a new pair on a pin at hole No. 3. Work them with the workers, remove and replace the pin with the stitch just made behind it (henceforth this will be summarised: 'Hang a new pair')

Work Full stitches to the left, through the pairs from Nos 3, 1 and 2. Hang a new pair at hole No. 4. Work back to the right through the pairs from Nos 4, 2, 1 and 3. Hang a new pair at hole No. 5.

Work Full stitches to the left, through the pairs from Nos 5, 3, 1, 2 and 4. Hang a new pair at hole No. 6. Work back to the right through the pairs from Nos 6, 4, 2, 1, 3 and 7, leaving out a pair at No. 5.

Work Full stitches to the left through the pairs from Nos 7, 1, 2, 4 and 6. Hang a new pair at hole No. 8. Work back to the right through the pairs from Nos 8, 6, 4, 2, 1 and 9, leaving out a pair at No. 7. This is the first resting place for the Trail. We must now set in the Ground.

The Ground

The two rows of Ground at the beginning of this pattern are worked from left to right (Nos 10–13 and 14–18), so that we put all the bobbins on in one go. For the rest of the pattern the Ground is worked in the usual direction, from right to left.

Hang a new pair on a pin at hole No. 10. Work these with the pair from No. 5: Full stitch, remove and replace the pin, Full stitch, twist twice. Hang a pair on a pin at hole No. 11 and work with the right hand pair from No. 10. Hang a new pair on a pin at hole No. 12 and work with the right hand pair from No. 11. Hang a new pair on a pin at hole No. 13 and work the right hand pair from No. 12. This leaves two pairs hanging on No. 13.

Go back to the pairs from Nos 7 and 10. Work these into hole No. 14. Work the pairs from Nos 14 and 11 into hole No. 15. Work the pairs from Nos 15 and 12 into hole No. 16. Work the pairs from No. 16 and the left hand pair from No. 13 into hole No. 17. Work the pairs from Nos 17 and the other pair from No. 13 into hole No. 18. Now the pairs for the Ground are all on.

Continuation of the Trail

Return to hole No. 9 to carry on working the next part of the Trail. With the workers, work Full stitches to the left from No. 9 across 4 pairs to hole No. 19. Twist the workers twice and put in the pin. This leaves out a pair at No. 8, ready for the Fan. Work back to the right from No. 19 through 4 pairs and pick up a pair at No. 20 (that is just as you did at hole No. 5).

Work Full stitches to the left from No. 20 across 4 pairs to No. 21. Twist the workers twice and put in the pin. This leaves out a pair at No. 19. Work back to the right from No. 21 through 4 pairs and pick up a pair at No. 22.

Carry on in this way until hole No. 27 is reached: working four pairs to the left and leaving pairs out for the Fan at holes Nos 21, 23 and 25; working 4 pairs to the right and picking up pairs from the Ground at holes Nos 24 and 26. Leave the workers to rest at No. 27, while you make the Fan.

The Fan

Hang two pairs on a pin at hole No. 28. Keep the first pair to the left. Work a Full stitch, remove pin from No. 28 and replace it with the stitch just made behind it, Full stitch, but only twist them once. With the right hand pair as the workers, Full stitch and twist with the pairs from Nos 8, 19, 21 and 23. Pin in hole No. 29. Remember to twist twice when turning round a pin. Full stitch and twist through 5 pairs back to hole No. 30.

Full stitch and twist 4 pairs to hole No. 31, and back again to No. 32.
Full stitch and twist 3 pairs to hole No. 33, and back again to No. 34.
Full stitch and twist 2 pairs to hole No. 35, and back again to No. 36.

Now the 'tongue'! Full stitch and twist 6 pairs to hole No. 37. This will take in the pair from No. 25. Work back: Full stitch and twist 6 pairs to No. 38.

Complete the Fan, working 2 pairs from No. 38 to No. 39, and back to No. 40. Full stitch and twist 3 pairs from No. 40 to No. 41, and back to No. 42. Full stitch and twist 4 pairs from No. 42 to No. 43, and back to No. 44. Full stitch and twist 5 pairs from No. 44 to No. 45, and back to No. 46. This completes the Fan. Leave the workers and one pair at No. 46 ready for the next Fan. The other pairs must now be picked up in the Trail.

Continuation of the Trail

Go back to the workers left at No. 27. Work 4 pairs to the right from No. 27 and pick up the pair from the left of pin No. 18 into hole No. 47. Work back to the left 5 pairs from No. 47 and pick up the pair from No. 37, into hole No. 48.
Work 5 pairs to the right from No. 48 to No. 49, leaving a pair out at No. 47. Work back to the left 5 pairs from No. 49 and pick up a pair at No. 50. Work 5 pairs to the right from No. 50 to No. 51, leaving a pair out at No. 49. Continue in this way, picking up pairs at Nos 52, 54 and 56; leaving out pairs for the Ground at Nos 51, 53 and 55. Leave the workers to rest on a pin at hole No. 57.

The second Ground

This is worked in the usual way, from right to left, working one pair less each row. There are five rows to work. Complete the Ground.

To continue

Make the next piece of Trail, then the next Fan. Make the next piece of Trail then the Ground. Continue in this way to the end of the pattern, and set up so that you are ready to turn the corner.

The corner

As in all patterns, part of the Ground is missing. Make the Ground as far as the corner diagonal. The Trail must taper off to a point. This means you will leave off pairs at both sides, when coming to the corner. It will be just like working the second half of the Cloth stitch Bud you made in the fourth pattern. There will be two pairs left at the last pin. One pair on the right will go straight across the corner. The pair on the left will be used in the 'tongues' of the two Fans that make the corner.
The Fans turn the corner in the same way as the Fans in the third pattern. Make two Fans one after another. It strengthens the corner if you twist the workers twice after each stitch in the corner section between the two 'tongues'. When the two Fans are complete, take the pair from the 'tongue' of the second corner-Fan and work this with the pair from the tip of the old Trail to make the first Full stitch of the new Trail (at No. 1). The left hand pair will be the workers. Use these to work the next Trail, which starts like the Cloth stitch Bud, by picking up pairs from both sides. Work the two rows of Ground from left to right, as at the start of the pattern.

To finish off

When all four corners have been turned, work an overlap row across holes Nos 1, 2, 4, 6 and 8. Then across holes Nos 1, 3, 5, 10, 11, 12 and 13.

CONCLUSION

I hope you have succeeded in making a satisfactory job of the six patterns in this book, and that you are now feeling ready to be more adventurous. There are thousands, maybe even millions of lace patterns to make, with different Fans, Grounds, Buds, Trails and stitches. It will take more than a lifetime to work them all so lose no time. There are many more books with patterns to work. Contact other lace makers; they will soon show you how to put in the bits I have left out, and will supply you with information to keep you hard at it in the years to come. Happy lace making.

SELECTED LIST OF BOOKS ON LACE

History

A history of lace, Mrs Bury Palliser, E.P. Publishing.
The romance of the lace pillow, Thomas Wright, Ruth Bean.
Pillow lace in the East Midlands, Charles Freeman, Luton Museum and Art Gallery.

Further Torchon lace manuals

Pillow lace, books 3 & 4, Margaret Hamer and Kathleen Waller, M.Hamer, Bedford.
The technique of Torchon lace, Pamela Nottingham, Batsford.

Manuals containing several types of lace

The technique of bobbin lace, Pamela Nottingham, Batsford.
Pillow Lace, A practical Hand-book, Elizabeth Mincoff & Margaret Marriage, Ruth Bean.

GLOSSARY

BUD   A geometric shape, usually diamond, round or oval.

CLOTH STITCH   A series of Full stitches made by a pair of workers across several passive pairs: in effect a piece of simple weaving.

FAN   A shape, usually the sector of a circle, worked on the outside edge of the lace.

FOOTSIDE   The straight edge of the lace, which is joined to the mounting material.

FULL STITCH   The main lace-making stitch, made with two pairs of bobbins: Cross the centre pair, left over right. Twist the outside pairs, right over left. Cross the centre pair, left over right.

GROUND, TORCHON GROUND,   The Ground is the net-like open work background to the lace. In this book we use Full stitch Torchon Ground.

HALF STITCH   The first two moves of Full stitch, i.e., cross the centres: twist the sides.

HEAD (repeat)   One complete repeat of the pattern.

HEADSIDE   Curved edge of lace opposite the footside.

INKING IN   The drawing in (after pricking) of all the lines which show the movement of the bobbins.

'LEG'   A pair of bobbins left out from one part of the lace waiting to be picked up in another.

PASSIVES   Pairs of bobbins remaining on the edges of the lace (on both footside and headside).

PICKING UP   Taking a pair from one part of the lace for use in another part.

PRICKER   A tool for pricking out patterns which can be made by putting a No. 8 or 9 needle, eye first, into a cork or pin vice.

PRICKING OUT   The transfer of a paper pattern on to stronger working material using a pricker (q.v.).

SETTING IN   Starting the pattern off.

SETTING UP   Moving the lace from the end of the pattern back to the beginning to allow the work to continue.

SPANGLE   A ring of glass beads, threaded on brass wire, attached to the end of the East Midlands type bobbin to add weight.

TRAIL   A series of threads worked in either Full or Half stitch making a continuous zig-zag or curved pathway through the lace.

WORKERS   A pair of bobbins which work continually from side to side across the lace (while other bobbins are used in turn).

SUPPLIERS OF LACEMAKING EQUIPMENT

Great Britain

D.J. Hornsby, 149 High Street, Burton Latimer, Northants.
Tel: Burton Latimer (053672) 2791.
A. Sells (Mrs), 49 Pedley Lane, Clifton, Shefford, Beds. Tel: Hitchin (0462) 814725.
Bedford Lace, 4 Newnham Street, Bedford. Tel: Bedford (0234) 57154.

United States

Robin & Russ Handweavers, 533 North Adams Street, Mcminnville, Oregon 97128.

Belgium

Manufacture Belge de Dentelles S.A., 6 Galerie de la Reine, Galeries Royales St Hubert, 1000 Bruxelles. Tel: 511.44.77.
't Handwerkhuisje, Marie-Paule Van de Pitte, Katelijnestraat 23, 8000 Brugge, Tel: 050 338129.